Tuning In To Spirit

Patricia Conte-Nelson

with the

Beloved Guides

Volume 1

This book supports you in tuning in to your Spirit.

First Edition 2017

Patricia Conte-Nelson

patriciaoneness@me.com

patriciacontenelson.com

ISBN-13: 978-1976146534
ISBN-10: 1976146534

I have been a Licensed Unity Teacher since 1992; past Spiritual Leader of Unity Fellowship Church in Norwalk, Connecticut; Wedding and Celebration of Life Officiant; Oneness Awakening Trainer; Prayer Chaplain at Unity on Cape Cod in Hyannis, Massachusetts and most recently an Interfaith Minister. It gives me great pleasure to serve the Divine in these ways and to share this book with you.

These Writings and the Beloved Guides

I began receiving guidance through Stream of Consciousness Writing in answer to my questions back in 1984. Stream of Consciousness Writing is free flowing. I do not stop to put in punctuation; I just keep writing or typing. After the Writing is complete, I go back and punctuate and paragraph.

I was told by a Medium who did psychic readings that I had Spiritual Guides who wanted to work with me, and I should listen to and write down what they said. The Medium told me to start by saying a protective prayer. I chose the Lord's Prayer.

A couple of days after my meeting with the Medium, I sat down to receive what I called a "Writing." When nothing came, I had a thought: "Write the Lord's Prayer." I was just saying it; I was not writing it. It was a quiet ah-ha thought that came out of nowhere; and I realized how powerful writing the Lord's Prayer would be. By the third time I wrote the Lord's Prayer, guidance started coming through. My chattering mind quieted as I focused on writing the words of the Lord's Prayer. From then on that has been my practice. I have continued to receive thoughts streaming into my mind to write an answer to any questions I ask.

A few years ago, along with the Lord's Prayer, I started each Writing by including the words, "I honor the Light within me. I am a clear and perfect channel. Divine Light is my Guide."

When I first started, I handwrote everything in spiral notebooks. Eventually I began to type the guidance I received, and to address the Spiritual Guides as "Beloved

Guides" or "Beloveds."

These Writings are a compilation of some of the answers I received from the Beloved Guides as well as Writings I wrote directly. The Beloved Guides reminded me there was no distinction between what is from them, and what is from me, and what is from both of us in any given Writing.

Their exact words are: *"It is all from the Divine within you. We have been helping you to go within to listen to the guidance, which comes from the Divine within you at the core of your Being. It is that guidance that you have been hearing all these years. It is all the Divine; even the reflections that you have made have been colored by your Divine Self."*

DEDICATION

For the Beloved Guides who have been with me since 1984 through thick and thin, sharing their words of wisdom. They are always there for me. Thank you, Beloveds. Without you these Writings and this book would not have come into being.

For Myrtle Fillmore and her profound book, *Healing Letters*, that I was guided to read decades ago in the middle of the night, which brought me relief during a dark night of the soul. She is lovingly called "Mother of Unity" and is the co-founder with her husband, Charles Fillmore, of the Unity movement.

For my mother, Stella Conte, whose words, "Don't die with your song unsung," helped bring this book to fruition. It is a part of my soul's song. Thank you, Mom. This is for you and everyone who has a song to sing.

For my wonderful husband, Bob Nelson, who has been the wind beneath my wings, my own special angel, helping me to fly. His unconditional love has always encouraged me to follow my heart.

ACKNOWLEDGMENTS

Right from the beginning I have been blessed by so many dear family and friends who have loved me and encouraged me to complete this book, and I am grateful to each of you.

Connie Farley, for all her love and wisdom and for helping me edit and create this book. She supported me in bringing it to completion. It was a joy re-reading the Writings together.

Jackie Woodside, for her amazing Life Design Course, books and wonderful inspiration along the way in so many ways. She taught me how to manage my energy rather than my time.

Angelic Master Teacher, Angelus, for his answers, in the form of spiritual messages, to my questions on the book.

Missy Kalat, for her invaluable revisions throughout the final drafts of the Writings and her loving support.

Liliana Cryer, for her love and friendship and graphic wizardry in formatting this book. She is one of God angels, who just happened to cross my path at the right and perfect time.

Beth Carleton, for the wisdom and beauty in your Angel Readings. Thank you for always being there.

Deep gratitude and love to my family for always loving and believing in me and the Writings, starting with my husband, Bob Nelson; and including my sister, Carolyn Pistey; my brother, Ron Conte; my nieces and nephews; my goddaughter, Carma Pawlewicz; and my long-time friend, Carol Mercer Penman. You have all been there with me.

Thank you to all of you who choose to read this book. I pray you love reading the Writings as much as I have loved writing the guidance I received. It has been a labor of love. May it help you to tune in more deeply to the Spirit within and to live life with more grace and ease.

Most importantly, thank you, God and Beloved Guides for continually inspiring me to be a channel for these Writings. It continues to be one of the greatest joys of my life.

FOREWORD

Many spiritual insights have come to me through the years as I have walked in my favorite places. One such place where I walk several times a week is the cranberry bog at the foot of our street where we live on Cape Cod in Massachusetts. I have always been blessed to live near beautiful scenic areas to walk.

Since walking is one of my favorite things to do, I have had plenty of opportunity to receive many messages and insights. On a walk many years ago, I saw a crow flying overhead with a baby bird in its beak. Heartbroken and angry, I cried out to God, "Why is it this way?" I heard, "Because I am the baby bird and I am the crow." This has been a difficult one for me to accept, and yet at the same time, I know it to be true. The Spirit of the Divine, God, the Source of all that is, lives in and as everything.

I read somewhere, "There is no spot where God is not." Remembering this gives me comfort and peace of mind in the face of everything that is going on in the world today. I trust there is a higher plan that I can't see right now, which is evolving under all the opportunities and the challenges.

My mission is to maintain the high watch in the midst of everything that is occurring, to not get sidetracked into judgment, to keep an open mind and heart, and to be humble, so that I may see clearly the Truth that all things work together for good in the end.

For me, I am learning that humility comes in the form of my being receptive to all experiences, without judging them, so I can continually see the connection, the Oneness, in everything.

I hope I've passed this on to you in this book. I would be delighted to have you share with me your experiences with this book. I can be contacted at patriciaoneness@me.com. Please start the subject line in the email with the word Book.

Love and gratitude, Patricia

PREFACE

My way of life tune in to Spirit. Since the early 1980's I have been tuning into the Divine, receiving guidance and direction from the spiritual messages I received from the Beloved Guides, and sharing them with friends. As a result, I have boxes of spiral notebooks in the basement of my home. It has always given me a deep feeling of fulfillment to tune in and connect to Spirit through these Writings.

Envisioning a dream is easy; following and manifesting it are not as easy. For many years, I have been dreaming about writing a book to share the Writings, and I have continually put it off as I pursued other endeavors. I almost got started on-line a few years ago when a dear friend, Ginny Caroselli, helped me post some Writings from Archangel Michael that I shared with her. She even found a picture of him to put at the top of the Writings. But I didn't follow through with it, and so it fell by the wayside.

At one point another dear friend, Donna Franklin, had the brilliant idea that I should write a blog for the Writings, which rekindled a spark in me, and I could feel the excitement of doing this rising. Spirit was taking no chance that I would let this fall between the cracks because Donna was inspired to create the blog, www.patriciacontenelson.com, that very afternoon, so that I could post Writings from the Beloved Guides immediately. As you can see, the Divine was working overtime providing all the help I needed to get started.

I received guidance from the Beloved Guides that it would take too long for the whole book-publishing process and that it was important that the wisdom in the Writings be available as soon as possible. I listened, and the idea for an eBook was born, which then turned into this book. Rather than the daunting idea of writing a book, I could actually envision something small like an eBook; and that made all the difference.

As I was considering all of this, I received a newsletter. The first sentence said, "As we enter this month, might I suggest that if you have been looking to start a whole new scene for yourself, then this is the month to do it. I don't care what it is that you are looking for…"

Well, there you have it, how all this got started with a little help from my friends, as that great song from the Beatles said. Or shall I say, with a lot of help from my friends, both on this side and the other side.

So here goes Volume 1.

How to Engage with These Writings

Here are several suggestions on how you can engage with these Writings:

- Read from beginning to end.
- Look at the Table of Contents and read any topic that interests you.
- Ask a question and randomly open to a page to receive guidance in answer to your question.
- Randomly open to a page and see what guidance you receive.
- If you are in the middle of an emotional upset, shift the emotion you are feeling by opening to a random page to receive an uplifting message.

As you can see, this Tuning in to Spirit is a wonderful resource to turn to as needed or as a spiritual practice for your life. Whether you are a beginner or whether you already have a spiritual practice, it can be a companion.

CONTENTS

LOOK AROUND YOU

If you stay aware, a wonderful gift will find its way to you; a person, a book, a course, a word, something, even a billboard will capture your attention and be a bit of guidance that will show you what track you have been on. At that point, you can decide if you want to change your life and choose a new way of being.

That is just what happened to me. One day back in 1982 I was visiting my sister and saw a book on the coffee table. My life at that point seemed to have fallen apart. Actually, it took falling apart for my life to come together in a new amazing direction. I reached out for the book and was mesmerized by it. My sister had bought the book thinking it would be a good read, but it did not resonate with her, so she left it there, thinking one of her Reiki clients might want to read it. It sat there until I visited a few months later and picked it up. That's how it was orchestrated for me to receive the guidance that would change the course of my life.

The way it happened was that my sister was walking through a bookstore, and the book literally fell out of the book stack onto her foot, so she decided to buy it. The name of the book is *Three Magic Words* by Uell S. Anderson. The three magic words the title refers to are "I AM God," which was a key revelation for me. It moved me deeply, and totally opened my mind to a new way of thinking and my eyes to a new way of seeing.

Opportunities like that abound. People like my sister, who was a conduit for me to receive the book, are all around us. My sister said to herself, "This book fell on my foot, and there must be something here," so she bought it. She had no idea at the time it was for me. But she followed her guidance

Can you see how it works? All is working together, and when you have the eyes to see, you begin to realize life is filled with wonderful opportunities. Open your eyes and look around you and see the next opportunity, the next synchronicity that has been planned for you, and act on it.

You are loved with an everlasting love.

CHOOSE TO EXPERIENCE "WHAT IS"

Tuning in daily is about connection to the Divine Presence that lives and breathes in every being. The Divine has a plan to be expressed through your unique being. It is special for each person.

Life is easier when you tune into the Divine Presence daily. You will receive your marching orders for the day, that which is yours to accomplish for that day. Each of you is like a river with a current. You have a course, a way of living your life with grace and ease, which is the path of least resistance. When you meet constant resistance all along the way, you know you are paddling upstream, bucking the current, resulting in feeling alone and separated from your divine nature.

When you resist "what is," whatever you are resisting persists. You are giving whatever you are resisting your energy and continue to attract it. Being in the present and experiencing "what is" without resistance is key. Look below the surface of what is showing up in your life that you resist. You constantly receive insights from your divine nature and the insights show you a more flowing way to live your life. Being in the present moment, the Now, is about seeing the insights as they unfold and allowing them to continue to unfold. You interfere and block your insights when you hold onto thoughts that things should look and unfold a certain way. When you refuse to experience "what is," the flow stops and you are again paddling upstream against the current.

Choose to experience "what is" with an open heart, embrace it and simply be with it. Proceed at your own pace, knowing guidance is there in every moment. You are never alone; Spirit is always with you sending you angels every step of the way to guide and direct you.

YOUR DAILY RADIO STATION TO DIVINE WITHIN

"What lies behind us and what lies before us are tiny matters compared to what lies within us."
Ralph Waldo Emerson

Everyone can seek within for their own guidance as channels for the Divine to flow through. Sit quietly and listen to what is received. Writing is helpful because it will help you to remember the guidance. It is there for you to read again and again and learn by taking it in deeply at a heart level.

To move out of the head and into the heart is the first key to receiving guidance. After you open yourself to receiving guidance by sitting in the silence, you will "hear" thoughts flow into your consciousness.

As you write, these thoughts will keep coming. Just sit and do not move from the spot of listening and writing. When the mind is busy listening, focused in the present moment, divine wisdom can flow through. Guidance is a fingertip away. It flows through your pen out of the Mind of God directly into your heart. Sit and listen. The key is sitting long enough to hear. Writing will quiet your mind and keep you focused on the Divine connecting with you from within.

Ultimately, this is the focus of everyone's life. Thus, life flows with grace and ease from within. So often, the human mechanism gets caught up in making things happen in the external world to the exclusion of the internal world. This external focus leads to busyness, which can carry you far from your inner guidance. Then you are subject to this world of appearances all around you, forgetting you are Spirit. You believe you are your thoughts and emotions. You think you are this being who is rushing from one thing to the next, wearing yourself out believing the world around you is your reality. You watch your little self, which is trying to juggle all the balls until you fall in exhaustion, finally realizing you can no longer go on this way. The real part of you is not that busy, harried being. It is the calm, peaceful, joy-filled flow of the Divine within you, so simply tune in. Tune your daily radio station to DIVINE WITHIN and go there often. Operate out of that radio frequency, which is always transmitting itself to you and through you. When you stop being so busy with external things, you will be happy to focus more within. You will not only see the benefits derived from this, but you will feel so good that you will want to return to it more often until it is your constant state of consciousness.

Your frequency dial will be tuned in to this station of inner peace, rather than being filled with the effort of trying to keep so many balls in the air at the same time. Let them all drop and see what emerges. It will emerge at a slower and calmer pace; you will see your life flow in harmony. Others will show up to help you without you trying to make it happen yourself.

So, enough for now! Go and practice this way of being, and it will be second nature for you to move through your life with grace and ease.

KEEP IT SIMPLE AND SURRENDER

I watched something beautiful and timely happen. I had been feeling disturbed for a couple of days about whether to do something or not. Originally, I had decided not to do it and felt good about my decision. Then I woke up the next morning second-guessing my decision, telling myself all the reasons why that was a bad idea. It really felt upsetting and I could see my ego was invested in the second scenario. I spoke to a dear friend who pointed out the original decision served me better than the second guessing, which would complicate my life when I am looking to simplify as much as possible. She pointed out where I was not choosing to support that by switching courses now. If I was really serious about simplifying my life, I needed to surrender and let it go.

The next day I was watching two little birds starting to build a nest in a potted plant we have behind the grill on our back deck. My husband, Bob, pointed out that was not a good idea because of the heat from the grill, and how upset the little birds would be when he was at the grill. So, I temporarily moved the pot inside to discourage them from continuing to build, and they were most upset, loudly chiding me from a nearby branch.

The thought came to me that the scenario with the birds is a perfect example of me. Spirit could see clearly what was for my highest good of living a simplified, uncomplicated life, and I had actually followed the guidance received. Then my doubting self stepped in to complicate it, and I was second-guessing my original decision. That was me chiding Spirit that had guided me to keep it simple and surrender.

My Spirit can see the future and knows what will happen when I complicate my life, just as I can see what will happen to the birds next time we use the grill. They are angry at me because they don't know that. How often have I been needlessly upset in the same way?

BEING IN STILLNESS IS OUR OXYGEN MASK

We have been receiving a huge influx of Light for some time. It is a powerful time for us, and there is more light and energy available to do our spiritual work than ever before.

We have the opportunity to do some major karmic clearing. It can bring up feelings of panic, which is just old stuff coming up to be cleared. It can bring on extreme exhaustion, which is the body absorbing and recalibrating the new vibration; so lying down and resting will help the body experience it with grace and more ease.

Since we are aware of what is going on, we

don't have to take it personally and assume there is something wrong with us. Instead we can create the habit of flowing with it and resting. The pace is being picked up even more energetically, so it's important to have the habit of taking as much time for stillness and spaciousness as possible, so we don't get overwhelmed. It is a matter of allowing us to be emptied in our quiet prayer time as we surrender everything to the Divine and feel the spaciousness of that. We can breathe into this clearing energy, and let it flow in us.

We don't have to experience it as slamming into us, which is how many experience the world around us. If we are coming from stability and stillness, we can open to it, rather than getting overwhelmed. Staying centered in this way will help us to help others who may be feeling overwhelmed by the energy of so much coming up to be cleared.

If we don´t feel spiritually connected ourselves, we have nothing to offer others. So, our first step is to put on our own oxygen mask without getting out of breath ourselves, just the way we do on an airplane so we can see clearly what our next step is.

We can prepare and hold the intention that

we are as open and clear as possible so we can be channels for this energy to flow through for ourselves and for others. Being in stillness and spaciousness is our oxygen mask. Through stillness and spaciousness, we will know what is ours to do.

You are loved with an everlasting love.

CHOOSE AN UPLIFTING MEMORY

Children of God, Light Workers, Beacons of Hope, whatever resonates with you, remember your magnificence and your mission to wake up and share it. What is your desire? You have it in your power to manifest by focusing on the amazing being you are.

You are energy that emits a vibration, which attracts to you what you are resonating with. If something you desire appears to be missing in your life, it is right there in the fullness of the Light you already are. So how to reveal it is the question, you ask.

Dwelling on what makes you happy changes your vibration. Even in the midst of difficult circumstances, choosing an uplifting memory raises your vibration. Your Spirit will soar, and move up, depending on how receptive you are to feeling uplifted.

Lift your mood to the vibration of what you are looking for. Look at the love you have in your life. Being in nature is filled with the vibration of love from the plant kingdom; being aware of babies, children, pets, birds chirping and soaring in the sky; stars that twinkle; the sun that shines and the brilliant moon.

There is so much around you to appreciate. You can feel gratitude for your magnificent body with multitudes of cells all working together in harmony.

What can you do today to have vibrant health that will make you more comfortable in your body? Go within for a few moments, and be with Being, which is pure perfection already. No place to run to, because right within you is the most magnificent healing spa in the world.

As you sit in the light of this magnificence that is always radiating within you, healing flows through your entire being. It is filled with warmth as it moves through every cell of your body, every thought in your mind and every feeling in your soul. All of this is going on right this minute in you now. As you are reading this, there is a world within and all around you. Your reminder is to be aware; just the thought of being aware and opening yourself to it raises your vibration.

You are loved with an everlasting love.

SPEAK TO US OF LOVE

Many are feeling more reactive, more judgmental, so the Beloveds speak to us of love in this writing:

Love is living in the heart, which is pure love, not romantic love, which can be colored by the ego and comes and goes. Divine love is eternal and does not come and go.

Behind the old patterns and beliefs is love, what you truly are. At a heart level, there is only the radiance of true love – Oneness with all that is. There is only the One, living out of everything, experiencing Itself over and over in all Its creations.

When you have a tendency to judge, remember this about yourself: you are love, and so is everyone else. You may not appear to be love, but it is who and what you are, whether you know it or not. You cannot change that Truth about yourself, for it is always there behind everything, so give not your attention to whatever appearances are manifesting that look unlike love.

It is not the Truth of who you are, so why waste time thinking about it or wishing you were not acting or being that way. It shows up so you may be aware of it and then choose the highest road. If you choose the lower road, fear not, for it will come again for you to choose the highest road. Ultimately you will, so don't worry about being on the right road. That only makes you unhappy and manifests it even more.

Your Divine nature is there, so choose to see it. You are offered many views to choose from, so choose. If it feels like the highest good for you at the time, be glad; if it feels like the lowest, be glad. What matters is your awareness of how you feel, which helps determine if you make that same choice again.

If you bury your feelings with addictive substances, be it food, drugs, alcohol or anything else, you stuff your emotions and then do not learn from them. Your feelings offer you the gift of experiencing where you are. Are you feeling connected or disconnected from your Divine Source? Feeling connected brings feelings of joy and peace; feeling disconnected brings feelings of depression and emptiness, and on and on. Becoming aware of your feelings, you can embrace and learn from them, using them as a path to the Divine within you.

Your core is love, which is where we began this Writing. So, remember no matter what you are feeling, it is all good. That is why you are here in the physical; to feel, to evolve, to remember your divine nature, to be in joy, to be the Divine consciously in physical form.

You are right on track, so have no fear you are falling behind. There is no behind. There is only the NOW; and in every moment, you are the Divine. You are love, and all is well, no matter how you are feeling.

You are loved with an everlasting love.

SPIRIT WORKS IN THE MOST
AMAZING WAYS

I read something about a man who was about to jump off a bridge. As he jumped, he realized everything he was concerned about could be fixed, except his jumping.

What did I have to learn from that? It made me stop and think about my own concerns and how I can choose to be with them. They are all opportunities to be fully present in each situation and allow them to be as they are and grow through each experience. The Oneness Blessing has helped me with allowing things to be as they are, awakening to the Divine within us. Each of us has that opportunity. Right here and right now, we are awakening to the Oneness in this moment, one with all there is.

In the midst of the external world is the foundation of Oneness that already is and has always been and always will be.

Each of us is on our path, and we are remembering our connection with one another in oneness and love. In this way, we begin to plant the seeds of love and compassion. We bring our own experience of the Divine as our gift to the Universe, our contribution to the One. A friend has a Science of Mind bracelet that says, "God is disguised as me." What a great reminder! In that consciousness, we can see the good in every situation. Ultimately, all works for the best and highest good. Even what appears to be a challenge on one level has hidden blessings for us, which we were not aware of when we were experiencing them.

When we have faith, our awareness grows, bringing with it patience and willingness to see from the highest perspective that God is in the midst of everything, as us, and within us. We see our relationships as opportunities to let go of our old ways of being and reacting. We see each situation as an opportunity to learn and grow. We no longer attract similar situations because we have finally learned the lesson that it's about what's going on inside of us, not only outside of us.

Spirit works in the most amazing ways. I have been asking for assistance to write more entries on the website. I received the idea to send a friend a short email, and it evolved into this entry. That's how life seems to work. We follow the guidance, and it leads to the next step.

You are loved with an everlasting love.

THE DIVINE'S MIDDLE NAME IS "SOMETHING"

At this busy time when it is so easy to get immersed in all that is going on around us, I find myself watching my patterns, points of view and perspectives that come up daily. There is always "something" there under it all, pushing at the boundaries of those old ways of being, so I can see everything in a new way.

I believe the Divine's middle name is "Something."

God/Spirit/Presence/Something is always there in us, expressing as us. In being available to listen to that "something," we can hear divine guidance, which is giving us a new perspective on the situation. Then we can make another choice to see things from

"Something's" perspective rather than our conditioned way of reacting, which can be biased.

In the midst of all the busyness, my challenge can be to be available to that "Something." When I am available, life flows more smoothly, and there is a feeling of inner peace and joy. I can always tell when I'm not being available because rather than experiencing peace and joy, I feel heavy inside.

If I don't listen to that Divine Something, I can quickly get lost in all kinds of thoughts about what is wrong with the world or "who done me wrong." Human conditioning is all around us. Thank God that more often than not these days, we listen and choose not to go into negative thinking. If (or should I say when) we find ourselves engrossed in negative thinking, the good news is we are not stuck there.

We can get out of our own minds. One of the best ways of getting out of our own negative thinking is to be grateful for what we do have, seeing the glass half full rather than half empty.

I had been thinking about this when I was buying Christmas cards. Not surprisingly, I came across a box of cards that quotes Philippians 4:8: *"Whatever is true, whatever is noble, whatever is right, whatever is pure, whatever is lovely, whatever is admirable — if anything is excellent or praiseworthy — think about such things."* Wonderful advice.

It's easier to live like this when we realize there is only One, and It is looking back at us in the mirror and in the face of everyone and everything around us. Good to remember when we are with family or with anyone we have difficulty with. It is always an opportunity to see with more loving eyes.

Abraham-Hicks reminds us that contrast is what we live with here on planet Earth, so we can feel the difference and make a choice about what we want to experience.

So, here's to feeling the contrast between our human perspective and the Divine Something and making a choice to be available to the Divine with gratitude that it never stops communicating with us. This is an auspicious time to plant the seeds of renewal and rebirth. Happy planting!

THE ENERGY HAS INCREASED

Namaste (I honor the Light within you),

You may be noticing the energy has increased and become even more powerful. We are moving deeper into the Golden Age, a time of peace, prosperity and happiness, as we awaken to our Oneness with all that is. What an incredible gift!

As you remember to ask and communicate with the Divine from moment to moment, life begins to flow and you find you are becoming more silent. The more silent you are, the more powerful your personal energy will become. Even upsets are short-lived, as you see there really is no "other" out there. There is only the Divine showing up in a myriad of forms.

As you have the eyes to see and the ears to

hear, you awaken to your Oneness, which shows up as kindness, compassion and understanding for everyone and everything. You experience deep abiding unconditional love and joy, which is your true nature.

You are loved with an everlasting love.

SYNCHRONICITY AND THE "STILL SMALL VOICE"

A little synchronicity showed up that I would not have been aware of if I had not paid attention to the "still small voice." Things like this happen around us all the time.

The "still small voice" (the voice of our Higher Power/God/Source/Divine Presence, whatever you want to call it) is always guiding and directing us on our path. There is also the voice of the mind, which speaks to us chattering away constantly with thoughts that don't always serve us. We can tell the difference because the "the still small voice" of our higher power uplifts us. The chattering mind voice that goes on and on can fill us with doubt. It constantly second-guesses us and others, causing us to feel fearful and distrustful. It certainly isn't uplifting. We're left feeling confused and let down.

So here is my latest uplifting moment with the "still small voice." It started when I received a phone call saying a dear friend had just been moved from the hospital to a local nursing rehab center.

The next day I received a phone call from someone who wanted me to officiate a wedding ceremony for him and his bride-to-be. When he called me back to finalize the date and time, I had just hung up the phone from speaking to the nursing rehab center where my friend had been moved. In the middle of our conversation, the groom mentioned that his bride-to-be worked at a nursing home. Something (the "still small voice") said it's the same place your friend is in. Ask him the name of the nursing home. As I have written before, I do believe "Something" is God's middle name. Yes, you have it by now. His bride-to-be works at the same nursing rehab center where my friend was just moved. He said he would ask her to check in on my friend throughout her stay, which she did daily. Now, how wonderful is that!

I love the amazing and mysterious way the Divine works behind the scenes, creating a harmonious way for everything to unfold. Our part is to stay in a state of awareness observing everything, paying attention to what is going on inside and the signs that show up around us. I became aware of how I was feeling as I thought about what happened, and I realized I was feeling happy, uplifted and peaceful, a sure sign that was the "still small voice."

You are loved with an everlasting love.

THERE IS ONLY THE ONE PRESENCE

Love:

There is no "I" or "other"
There is only the One Presence.
The Radiance of this Being
Now shining forth as
Who and What I AM.
Everything is the Presence.
Just be what is going on.

(This beautiful passage was shared with me by a friend. I am so grateful for it because it says it all. There truly is only One Presence living and breathing as us.)

TRUSTING BY FOLLOWING
THE GUIDANCE

A perfect example of TRUSTING is what happened to me when I had an appointment with an amazing man, who does a variety of body therapies. He had suggested the week before that I might want to meet a friend who is a Certified Herbalist. Since I am interested in learning more about the benefits of herbs, I planned to call her for an appointment, but had not gotten around to it yet. When I was in the therapist's office, who should show up but the herbalist at the exact time and place where I was. Divine timing brought us together without my having to try to make anything happen. I showed up and so did she.

An example of not trusting happened to

me many years ago with Barbara Marx Hubbard. She has written wonderful books and is a very well-known author and spiritual leader. I was at Unity School of Religious Studies continuing my Unity studies. I had brought her book with me, *The Revelation – Our Crisis is a Birth.*

I received guidance that morning that I should bring the book with me because I would run into her that day. I did not believe the guidance and left the book behind. Well, who should be standing in front of me in the cafeteria lunch line but Barbara Marx Hubbard. It turns out that she was a guest speaker that day for the ministerial students. I mentioned my early morning guidance and she said she would be happy to autograph the book for me. I told her I didn't have it with me, but that I would go to the bookstore next to the cafeteria and buy another copy. I returned with the book and she autographed it to me with the note, "Follow the Guidance." So, it did work out well in the end and taught me to listen to the guidance.

You are loved with an everlasting love.

SLOW ME DOWN, LORD,
SO I APPRECIATE LIFE

I have watched myself in the throes of what goes on many mornings. I was trying to drink my morning smoothie, while balancing some devotional books in my lap that I like to read to start my day, and popping up to take clothes out of the washer and put them in the dryer. I continued to drink my smoothie, stir the breakfast cereal, and read all at the same time. They have a name for this; it's called multitasking. Often, I multitask all through the day, as many of us do. It can be difficult to take any satisfaction in finishing one job and starting another when you're almost unconscious of what you're doing because you're doing so many things at once.

It came to me that it's very destructive to my peace of mind and enjoyment of life when I live like that. I don't give myself my full attention to focus in the moment on what I'm doing. It's how we can leave home, drive somewhere new, and wonder how we got there. It's only in the moment that we can be aware of what's going on around us, feel connected, and hear guidance from within.

If we're focused on several things at once, there is no spaciousness to hear the inner voice always speaking to us. We miss the grace that is flowing into our lives, showing us how to enjoy the moment. We miss feeling connected to what we're doing or how to get the most out of whatever we're doing.

For instance, how much more nutritious will my smoothie be if I'm savoring it and really tasting it and feeling that I'm doing something good for my body. In that moment of really tasting and savoring, I increase the nutritional value of whatever I'm eating or drinking because my body can assimilate it better if I'm calm and not stressed.

How much more will I absorb and enjoy what I'm reading if I'm not popping up and down doing something else at the same time. I don't have to go on; I think you get my drift here. Sometimes multitasking is unavoidable, but as a way of life, it can be harmful to our body, mind and Spirit.

My plan is to focus on one thing at a time and check in at the end of the day to see what the quality of my day was. I have a feeling it will be filled with more moments of inner peace, more happiness, and a less harried way of being. So, I can receive "those touches that delight the soul" and feel the joy of being touched by God, the Essence of our being, that Sri Aurobindo wrote about:

"The subliminal mind receives and remembers all those touches that delight the soul. Our soul takes joy in this right touching by the Essence of all experience."

Thank you, God, for breaking through and helping me to hear you speaking to me.

You are loved with an everlasting love.

CHOOSE JOY

"Joy cometh in the morning." Psalm 30:5. With every new morning there is the opportunity to choose joy.

We have all the power we need to create all the changes we choose. Joy can be a fleeting thing in this world here on Earth; and yet it is waiting around every corner for us to choose. Stress, too, can be waiting around every corner when we choose to worry or think things "should" not be as they are and we fight against it. The moment we resist "what is," we are stressed because resistance starts pumping emotions through our body about whom we should call, what we think we should do, what's on our plate for the day to do. It can be compelling because it is all around us in living color.

Our phone rings, our computer blinks its many messages about what's out there and what we need to do about it. Thoughts about going for a walk, sitting and relaxing, taking some time to read a book or looking out the window at the change of season, all fly out the window as our minds begin to race and we take on the pace of the day. This way of life feeds our stress level.

When we quiet our mind, and take a deep breath, we can choose to focus on the joy that is present, like an inner stream. Breathing in the peace and knowing that in the grand scheme of things all is well, is one of the greatest gifts we can give ourselves. We really don't have to have our hand in every pie that crosses our table. We can leave some for someone else and taste only that which calls to our deepest heart.

We have time for so much when we stop and take a moment to breathe in peace and release the stress. Take a moment now to close your eyes and breathe in, *"I am living a beautiful and fulfilling life. I am happy and at peace."* Even if it does not feel true right now, what would that look like for you? Feel that for a moment and keep breathing into it.

Have a lovely day and pick the pieces of pie that feed your soul and are truly for your highest good. Your heart will tell you so much because when you choose your highest good, your heart will sing with joy, rather than feeling oppressed and overwhelmed. In the long run, it will also prove to be for the highest good of others because you will choose whatever you decide to do from a place of love rather than resistance.

You are loved with an everlasting love.

EVERYWHERE YOU LOOK IS
A BIT OF GOD

When I was with my dear friend, Lydia, I saw a rainbow falling across her pregnant belly. The rainbow was a reminder of God's covenant with each of us. I heard God deep in my heart,

"Here! Here, is a little bit of Me. Here is a little bit of Me."

This is a Writing that I received from the Beloveds at that time:

As you look about you and see the Divine in everything, you feel a sense of peace. The hand of God is everywhere you look: in babies, in people, flowers, trees, butterflies, bees, birds, in all creatures. All are the hand of God showing up, reminding you that here is another little piece of Me. The feeling of peace settles into the deepest part of your being, as it dawns on you that everywhere you look is a piece of God. Even what appears in the world around you as chaos has a piece of God in it. Because as Light Workers, you have the opportunity to lift up everything you see into the Light by calling on the Divine in all circumstances. You bring your consciousness and the world to a higher place.

Rather than dwelling on what you see as negative, you can choose to raise your vision higher by seeing God smiling with eyes of love. You ask, *"How do I see God smile with eyes of love?"* Through the smiles you see on the faces of others, through the smile that looks back at you in the mirror, through looking out at nature that has been provided for your eyes and heart to rest upon in gratitude.

In feeling the Divine within, you hear, *"Here is a little bit of Me."* You remember, I AM God in Action; and with a sigh of gratitude you lift the world. You spread this little bit of God everywhere you go with everyone you meet. In this way, you make every day filled with love and light and empower others to follow their bliss into the heart of God.

OPEN TO THE DIVINE LIGHT

I love the way the Universe works. There is so much synchronicity all around us. As I sat at my desk to ask for a Writing I could share, I cleared away some papers. Under the papers, I found this message that I received from Archangel Michael some time ago. I realized that was what I was to share.

Beloved Archangel Michael, the message you shared was that you have much to say to those of us who will take the time to listen. I am listening.

Archangel Michael's message was:

It is a time of many repercussions circulating through the Earth due to tremendous unrest in the hearts of many. That is why it is imperative you keep your hearts at rest, rather than in a chaotic space focusing on the disturbances around you. Focus on the Truth of your being, your divine nature, love.

Many have been given the gift of insight, so use it well to awaken others to the Divine Light that they are. Anyone who wishes to do this work can tune in and open to the Divine Light, feel it circulate through their being, focus on the heart of love and radiate that to the planet.

Take time for love. Love is the reality of your being. So, allow yourself to be the channel for love to flow through you to the planet. How do you do this, you ask? As you focus your intention and attention within, you open to the Divine Light.

If you focus on the unrest in the outer world, you continue to create more of that in your life. Instead, choose to focus your attention on the Light within rather than the external chaos.

Even in the darkness, there is always the Light present, so focus your attention on the Light at the center of everything. The minutest amount of Light you can feel will help the planet and help you move out of the upsetting emotions you may feel. You feel that because there is so much of it in the world. Just being with it rather than pushing it away can overcome it. It comes that you love it, and love yourself as the Wholeness you already are.

As you push away parts of yourself that you consider unlike the Light, you fracture yourself, separate yourself into pieces of what you think is good and what you think is bad, and you negatively judge yourself. This serves no one, least of all you and creates a sense of separation. You cannot permanently separate yourself, but you can feel that way in the moment, which leaves you feeling bereft and empty. Then the Wholeness you are feels like it is a million miles away.

Your Wholeness is right here in the midst of you, healing and whole, doing its work. In any given moment, you are feeling the Presence of the Divine within, or you are feeling bereft in the world, adrift and lonely, or you are somewhere in between. Which can you feel in this moment as you read this message?

You can choose to feel the Divine Being you are. Open your heart to the message, and let it remind you that you are already whole, and you don't have to try to find it outside anywhere. To assist you with this, it can be beneficial to read uplifting material for it focuses you there, so that you feel the Light, absorb it, and walk consciously in the Light this day.

You are loved with an everlasting love.

HO'OPONOPONO, "CLEARING THE DECKS"

Dear Ones, this morning in meditation I was guided to work with an old Hawaiian Prayer: *"I am sorry. Please forgive me. I love you. Thank you."* It is called Ho'oponopono; and I said it for all those I had ever hurt and who had hurt me. Then during my Writing time, I asked the Beloveds what is my message for the day and this is what came to me:

You are already doing it. You are "clearing the decks" and asking for forgiveness from all those you may have offended, so continue the process.

Please know that in the big picture there is nothing to forgive. There are only people playing out their roles in life, learning as they go along. In the process of learning, they commit acts that are wounding to others. The quicker you are able to feel it, move through it to the other side, and feel love, the happier you will be. It will feel like the Sun is shining brightly inside you, and flowing out into the world.

Continue to love yourself, for you are the person you hold hostage with any feelings of unforgiveness you may hold onto. Instead, choose to release it now, or at least look at being willing to release it. The willingness will open the door to your heart, followed by feelings of love and joy. And that is why you are here... to feel and share the love and joy everywhere. As time goes on, the feelings of overwhelming love in your heart will flow and reach out and embrace all around you. You will feel more and more joy and freedom. Your heart is opening wider, and there is more room for the love to pour through totally unencumbered by old wounds, past hurt from others or towards others. Your feeling of freedom expands, and you are actually able to accomplish more with less effort because you have released the hurt or pain that was there. You are finally free, which frees your energy.

THE EYES OF LOVE

Recently I asked how could I best be of service?

I received this Writing from the Beloveds in answer to my question, and later that day, I read something beautiful about being of service. Don't you just love the way synchronicity flows all around us? I sincerely believe that synchronicity is simply the Divine in action in our lives.

There is a world filled with hurting people who just want some loving kindness, some attention paid to them, so they don't feel hopeless and alone. Loneliness is one of the biggest causes of desperation and depression. The body's need for love and attention is huge. When ignored long enough, many otherwise harmless diseases, which can pass on their own undetected, become exacerbated for lack of kindness, love and compassion. Simple caring goes a very long way toward helping the soul and the body to heal.

There is a simple word that you can use to assist others. "Attention" – pay attention to yourself, as you are paying attention to others. You feel better, they feel better. It is not time-consuming to pay closer attention. Not attention to all the imperfections you see with the human eye, but attention with the spiritual eye. You are a spiritual being, here to be aware of your divine nature, to help one another to remember that. You are not meant to pick one another apart with small imperfections, which can then turn into large imperfections in your eyes because of all the attention you focus on them. Viewing people though the eyes of perfectionism pulls people's energy fields down. Instead you can look out at the world through the eyes of love, and change the world one person at a time, by seeing what you love and focusing on that: a tree, a flower, a baby, a pet, anything at all that raises love in your heart higher than it was before. Stretch your love every day. Look with the same eyes that just saw love, and look at someone or something you have loved less in the past, and see them through the eyes of love, and watch love grow.

Watch yourself each day finding more things to love. Love is God in Action. It is the act of love that transforms a dreary day into an uplifting happy day. It transforms your mood from the inside out, and you find more to love. Through the Law of Cause and Effect, you send love out and love comes back. Maybe not from the person to whom you just sent love, but from another source. You are love at the core of your being. It's Who you are. So, let it out. Don't hold back. The more you hold back, the unhappier you are. So, for today, one day at a time, practice being love, even to what you have found unlovable in the past. May this add more love to your day, today, and every day.

You are loved with an everlasting love.

HEAVEN IS AN INSIDE JOB

At a time when I was having a lot of doubts, the Beloved Guides shared this with me:

We smile at your doubts because they are the very doubts others have about their worthiness and their purpose. There is no "supposed to." You came here to this realm to explore and experience, so go ahead and explore and experience. Above all, have fun doing it. Your Spirit is whole and intact already. Whatever you experience does not affect your inner Wholeness. You are always whole, no matter what the appearances.

So where do you go from here? You go to "Heaven." Heaven is an inside job. It comes from the depth of your being, from the indwelling Source of all life that lives in you, as you. Allow it to flow forth into your life. From that flow, Heaven is created right here on Earth.

Be at peace, knowing there is nothing to do, nowhere to go, and nowhere to be more than you already are. There is only the now moment. Fill it with joyful remembrance of the Divine Being you already are. Breathe in that realization, and it will transform your life into more simplicity and inner peace.

In every moment, your Divine Spirit enfolds you. Live in that knowing.

Don't let your fear keep you from us. We are your family of origin, your God-Self Family. There is nowhere to hide. There is only the All of us, and we are One.

You are loved with an everlasting love.

BE YOUR OWN BEST HEALER

Many internal blocks, whether they are physical, mental, emotional or spiritual, have something to do with regret about something you or someone else did or didn't do. The blocks can cause emotions, such as fear, depression, anxiety, guilt and lack of forgiveness for one's self and others.

These emotions and behaviors clog your guidance system. How can you hear guidance when you are tuned to the frequency of regret instead of the frequency of love and compassion for yourself and others?

Regret comes from NOT remembering you are a spiritual being visiting planet Earth in a suit of clothes called your body, experiencing life.

As soon as you feel regret, you can nip it in the bud by embracing your past self and realizing you did the best you could at the time. Take time to feel compassion, understanding and love for yourself. Say to yourself, *"Everything is all right. I love you. I care about you."* Be your own best healer. Don't wait for someone else to say it to you. Say it to yourself.

You are loved with an everlasting love.

LOVE YOURSELF

When I asked the Beloved Guides about some pain I was in, they shared this with me:

Love yourself. Send love to all the hurting places in your body. Whether it is physical, emotional, mental or spiritual, it is all the same. You are experiencing a physical pain. Ultimately, everything that is physical initially had its roots in some subconscious call from your body to slow down, to listen, and become aware of the ache in your heart, or somewhere in your being, where you may be holding on to something that it would be best to let go of.

You can push things down for just so long, even years, but eventually it will show up in some way.

Accepting yourself and life as it is helps.

When you block your flow of energy, of life force, from flowing through your body, eventually it creates a blockage wherever the energy is stuck and not flowing.

Energetically, you can even attract certain things to you that cause physical pain. No matter what it is, there is something behind it energetically. Changing your energy by sending love, understanding and compassion to that area helps the energy to start moving again.

Sometimes stronger measures are needed because the energy has been blocked and stuck for so long. Ultimately, attending to it and loving it is a major part of your healing process, so let the healing process begin now. Love, love, love, and more love for self, as well as all others, is the best prescription for healing.

You are loved with an everlasting love.

ASCENDING INTO THE LIGHT

Sometimes I feel like I have missed the boat with all the procrastination and divergent paths that have carried me far and wide. There are many like me. What would you share with us, Beloveds?

Here is their response:

There are many boats leaving the old consciousness for the new consciousness. There is no "missing the boat." There is only waking up to your soul's passion for ascending into the Light.

It is all around you, and within you. You have simply to become aware of it, to be conscious of it, and allow it to guide and direct you. You are always receiving messages. As you tune in daily, you become more adept at hearing and following your guidance. Your inner Self knows what is for your highest good.

No matter how many times you stop listening and get embroiled in what seems like a divergent path, the inner Self is still there, and you have learned on the divergent path what it feels like not to follow the voice of the inner Self. It is not good or bad, so do not name it so. Simply be aware of it, and move forward, surrounded, protected and filled with the Light of the inner Self, the Indweller of Light.

All is well, Children of the Light, for you are, after all, made of the Light. You are the Light that has come to planet Earth at this time of transformation to hold the Light for all. It is why you are here.

You are loved with an everlasting love.

GOODWILL AMBASSADORS

Beloved Guides, I think I am a Goodwill Ambassador. It came to me as I was remembering all the people I spoke to on the ferry to Martha's Vineyard and at the ferry terminal.

This is the response I received from the Beloved Guides:

How perceptive of you. That's exactly what you all are. You are here to spread goodwill; to share your open-hearted loving way of being with everyone you meet. Light Workers came to do just that; and along the way over human lifetimes, their Light became more and more hidden by fear of many things they encountered here on Earth. However, this is ending. Soon there will be enough awakened beings remembering their spiritual nature and why they are here, to cause the shift in awareness and awakening to move even faster.

There are many groups around the world offering free opportunities for people to join together on the phone, on the Internet and in other ways. Hearing words of Truth with an open heart will awaken them to remembering Who they are. These words of Truth will lift the fear that has kept them trapped in the material way of living, where the focus is on trying to stay alive with mortgages, jobs and other responsibilities. Fear has caused much discomfort in the body, which then adds health concerns to the list of things that keep them trapped, forgetting the Light within that is the true healer.

You have all been given the opportunity to move along with the shift, to catch the momentum of the group energy. It matters not which group you choose. What matters is that you choose, and not go meandering along, or allowing the fast pace of life to push you until you lie in bed at night wondering what happened to your day.

You have the opportunity to choose how you spend your day with the attitude you bring to it. Are you doing whatever it is consciously, be it mowing the lawn, washing dishes, or making corporate decisions? Are you doing it from the consciousness that you are a Being of Light, spreading love near and far? Everything becomes a Holy Experience when you live your life with this awareness. You transform not only your own energy field, but also that of the planet.

You are moving in this direction. How much peace, love and joy you feel each day depends on how much time you spend inundated in fear of your material circumstances, and what you think you need to do about it, how much harder you think you need to work. Can you see how thinking you need to do more and more keeps you trapped in this way of living? It keeps you in a lower vibrational frequency. This way of being keeps you from seeing the insights, intuitions and synchronicities all around you that will help you move forward on your path of remembering you are the love you want to see. As Jesus and other teachers and way-showers have shared, *"It is the Father's good pleasure to give you the Kingdom of Heaven."* So, you can choose to be Goodwill Ambassadors of love, peace and joy wherever you find yourself, even on the ferry to Martha's Vineyard.

You are loved with an everlasting love.

EXPERIENCE IT ALL
WITH A LOVING HEART

I asked the Beloved Guides, *"Why do I do what I don't want to do, and not do what I want to do?"* The following was their reply:

That is the perennial question, dear one. You are on the human level in a human body, with lots of deeply imbedded patterns that are working themselves out this lifetime.

Let it unfold as it will, and just be with it as it unfolds. Your experience of all of it, with awareness of what's happening, is key. You have for some time been "watching" this process with awareness of it. Continue to do so, remembering joy is why you are here. Joy is the greatest service you can provide to others and to this planet, for it has such a high vibration that it pulls everything else up with it. This is the master plan, and you are all participating in it valiantly. Day by day, you continue, and you do the best you can. This is all you can do.

Where improvement can happen is when you "see" what you have done or not done, be kinder to yourself, with the realization you are doing the best you can at a human level. This is important because your own vibration depends on it. You cannot be vibrating joy when you are telling yourself how you "should" have done or not done something in a harsh way.

You do what you do until you don't. Can you be okay with this? The more you feel you are doing something wrong, the more you are empowering it with your energy, and you keep it going. Let this writing be the healing it is meant to be.

Focus on the inner joy that is already within you, bubbling to the surface when you are not telling yourself you "should" do better. You can all be shining lights for one another by practicing self-acceptance and self-love by realizing you are the hands and feet of your God-Self. You are Divine, here to experience being human with all the patterns. So not wanting those patterns is a waste of your precious energy. Simply experience it all with an open, loving heart and you will see the transformation that is already within you.

You are loved with an everlasting love.

THIS IS A NEW DAY

Beloveds, would you please share a message as we enter the next phase of our lives. What would be good for us to focus on? The following was the reply:

Keep your heart open to what is already there, and what is pouring in to assist you. That will take care of everything for you. In the old way, what you focused on multiplied and came back to bless or haunt you. In the long run, it was all a blessing because you were able to see what you were doing by what showed up in your life. Sometimes you were aware of what you were doing, and you could see the repercussions immediately. At other times, it took a while for whatever you were unconsciously focusing on to show up. But show up it did, and many of those things are in your life now. Now is the time to let it all go, and to know there is a higher order of things; and you are benefiting from all of it.

So simply tune into what is already in your own heart. It will become more and more evident as time goes on that it does not behoove you to cry over spilt milk. This is a new day. Let the spilt milk go. Much has been released for you already. Be aware of the good all around you, and within you, and the good will continue to multiply.

Cease trying to figure things out or trying to fix yourself and everything around you. That is unnecessary work for you, and it just wastes your precious time and energy, which could be used to greater benefit by being in joy, actually enjoying every day.

As you move through your day, being conscious of just what you are doing, no matter what it is or how small, and when you are truly present to it, you stay in a place of gratitude for all of it. Your mood and your energy field will rise to match that joy and gratitude. That is the energy that is sweeping the planet from all sides, from all the Light Workers who are here awakening to their

Divinity no matter what it looks like in the world around you. Just remember the Truth that with God all things are possible and the Light will prevail.

You are loved with an everlasting love.

HERE TO GIVE AND RECEIVE LOVE

Where around you is there a need for what you have to offer, no matter what it is? You all have a special gift to offer the world with your loving attention to the simple act of loving wherever you are.

Rather than paying attention to what you don't have, it is really about seeing what is all around you. What do you have that can be shared with others: your time, your talent, your abundance, in whatever form that takes? These opportunities will present themselves to you in big and small ways.

Love and gratitude have always been there, and now they are present even more because people are awakening to the realization they are here to give and receive love. That really is our main purpose. Wherever you can allow more love into your own heart, say YES to all of it: a loving gesture, a kind word, a look of kindness or a smile. Whatever it is, nothing is too small to love and appreciate and to share.

The more this is practiced, the more love swells into the fullness of what it is, which is unconditional love; not for what someone does or doesn't do, but for the Divinity already in the person. All is Divine, so be in gratitude for all of it.

There is only God manifesting in many forms. When the realization of that truly bursts forth and flowers in your hearts, then you can see it really showing up in your lives.

You are loved with an everlasting love.

MAKE MORE CONSCIOUS CHOICES

The Beloved Guides shared this with me:

Forget not that the spiritual hierarchy is helping you. You are not alone, and you are being rewarded for the work you have done, just trying to keep your head above water while the world swirled around you. Sometimes the world's circumstances dragged you under, but you kept coming back to the surface for another breath of air to keep on going.

You are much more conscious now, and that very consciousness will help you see yourself as you move forward each day. When things aren't flowing, you catch yourself sooner, and back up, and start over again. Your consciousness will guide and direct your actions, your thoughts and your feelings. You will see this, and you will be more aware, and be able to make more conscious choices about how you want to be in any given moment, in any given situation, with any person.

So be at peace and know all really is in Divine Order, and today is the beginning of a new way of being, of living more consciously. Consciousness means simply being more aware.

You are loved with an everlasting love.

YOUR NEW WAY OF BEING

I was watching the squirrels that I feed in our backyard, who were chasing each other around, protective of the seeds I had just given them. I sent them a prayer, *"Come on, guys, share with one another. There is more than enough. I will give you more."* It reminded me of our relationship with the Divine. Following is the Writing I received from the Beloveds:

The Divine is in all. When the awareness of that comes to the heart, the heart is no longer afraid of lack and limitation of any kind.

You are inbred with your own set of beliefs, but alongside those beliefs, lying dormant within, awaiting your realization, is the awareness that you are a spiritual being and that all things are yours for the receiving.

What is the key to receiving all the wonderful gifts of the kingdom that the Divine has for you?

It is about letting go of what you think you already know to be true from your past experience, and simply allowing yourself the freedom to explore new ways of feeling about your life.

You are here to experience all that is, to see what it feels like to experience lack, limitation and abundance, all of it. Whatever it is simply is an experience. So, experience it all with no expectation or attachment to either way of experiencing something. Just observe how it makes you feel. You can then choose the way that makes you feel inner joy, contentment and peace. Allow yourself to experience or see what that feels like, and be with that for as long as it lasts.

New experiences will come, and you will see them in a different way, which you have now learned from your new way of being. Without expectation and attachment, everything can show up brand new for you, rather than with the old paint over it, which you have placed there with your past way of experiencing. In the past, you experienced every thing with your old eyes. Your spiritual eyes will create a whole new way of being for you, and thus a whole new life.

You are loved with an everlasting love.

CONNECTION TO
THE DIVINE WITHIN

Another message that the Beloved Guides shared with me:

When you look at the world around you with spiritual eyes, you feel more connected to the Divine within you, which helps you to feel more connected to everyone and everything around you. When that happens, you are more careful of how you treat everyone and everything, including your own body.

You will begin to make better choices about what you eat, drink, think and do. From that comes a whole new way of life. It happens one step, one awareness at a time, simply by being willing to experience your life in a new way, rather than the same old tired way that has not served your highest good or the world for a long time.

When you make a connection to the Divine, you awaken to the inner spark of Divinity that lives and breathes within you. Everything else becomes new because you are now living from that space of connection; separation falls away, and you remember you are One with all.

Of course, you would like to experience this quick way of awakening to the Divine within, but sometimes it is necessary to experience your life before this happens. The key is not to be attached to either way. It is that very attachment, trying to make it happen, that keeps you feeling separated from the Divine. In Truth, you are already Divine, so there is no need to try to make it happen.

"As long as you believe in and give power to the illusions of this world, you will get caught up in them. This isn't bad; it may be that the cause and effect with which you are dealing is going to hold you on the earth plane for a few more lessons, for a few more experiences. Love them." John Roger, DSS

You are loved with an everlasting love.

PAY ATTENTION TO
THE SYNCHRONICITIES

So many synchronicities are happening. Last night I had just gotten into bed, and I had the feeling that I had to do something in my office; I could not figure out what it was. It just felt important, so I got up and went to my office. I put a few things away, one of which was a book sitting on my desk that I had been guided to pull out a couple of days earlier, so it was still on my desk.

When I opened it, it opened to the perfect spot. Wow! That was an eye opener. It answered the question to something that had been on my mind for some time. What I read and the fact that my eyes just "happened" to fall on that book, which was still on my desk, were another realization that we are being helped all the time. Our part is to follow the guidance when it comes through, even when we're in bed. Guidance is always coming through.

In putting the book away, another book "caught" my eye, *The Light Shall Set You Free*, by Dr. Norma Milanovich and Dr. Shirley McCune. It opened immediately to Chapter 6, The Fifth Dimension. According to some teachings, the Earth and all beings living on the Earth are in the process of shifting into a whole new level of reality in which a consciousness of love, compassion, peace and spiritual wisdom prevails. This has been called the Fifth Dimension.

I have worked with Marconics, which is about the Fifth Dimension and beyond. How I met Alison David Bird, who started Marconics, is another amazing synchronicity in itself. I was guided to attend a convention where she was speaking. I had not planned to attend. I didn't even know she was there as a guest speaker. That morning I received guidance to go to the Health Expo in Marlboro, Massachusetts, which I did. That is where I met Alison and Marconics, and learned more about the Fifth Dimension and beyond, and so much more. It was a divine appointment for sure; and I am so grateful I had the opportunity to work with Alison.

I have been meaning for years to donate or sell some of my books and have not done it. Now I see that my books are my resource library. I never know what I will be guided to on any given day.

I asked the Beloved Guides if they would like to comment on these synchronicities, and the next writing, Listening is the Gateway to Hearing Guidance, is what came through.

You are loved with an everlasting love.

LISTENING IS THE GATEWAY
TO GUIDANCE

This Writing relates to the previous one about guidance and the Fifth Dimension, which I asked the Beloveds to comment on. Here is their reply:

It is not always entire books that you have to read. You may be guided to read only certain chapters. It is the realization of what happens when you listen to the guidance that is key. In the listening, you are connected to the Fifth Dimension and way beyond. The listening is the gateway to hearing guidance.

There is so much guidance being offered in every moment. Just listen! It's coming through all day and all night. In the listening, you save yourself from going around and round in the same potholes you have fallen into for years. Those are old outworn potholes filled with old patterns and beliefs, and you are ready to let them all go.

So, we are guiding you to new things every day, and you are all starting to really pay attention. Even if you do not follow through in that moment on what you read or what we share with you, the seed is there. Hours or days later, we see you doing something about it, which is how it works. We send guidance; and as you are ready to implement it, you do. Of course, without beating yourself up about how long it took you to implement it, which only retards your progress.

It happens when you are ripe for it; and ripeness is as different for each of you as it is for each type of fruit. So just go with whatever the timing is for you. Another person's timing may be different from yours, so why compare yourself? It is such a waste of time, and only causes you pain and suffering. Let go of the pain and suffering. It is time to be free and fly.

You are loved with an everlasting love.

ACTS OF TRUE LOVE

I see how financial concerns often govern so much of our lives on this planet. We seem to be so governed in this way that we are compromised in many decisions we make. I asked the Beloved Guides how can I be authentically me, the real me, without being compromised by the seeming needs that come up in considering decisions I make, and I received this answer:

Look at the face of the issue. What is it? It is fear of lack and limitation; fear that more money, or whatever, is needed to make you or someone else more whole, life more wonderful, and so on. Wholeness and everything you think you need is already within you. Look at all you have that is absolutely free.

Look at Mother Earth's love and what she provides for you: trees, flowers, birds, little critters, bees, food, water and so on. There is so much here for your enjoyment.

Look at the night sky. The beauty of the stars, moon, planets and the realization that there are Beings out there, all existing at the same time you are. There are Beings that are sending you light and love, helping and protecting you every step of the way. Right there, you have a huge gift that contributes to your well-being.

Now move on to the sun that keeps you warm and gives you the love it pours down on you every day. Even behind the clouds, it is beaming love to you, in the form of its warmth and light, which it gives of itself freely.

See your body, the intricate way it is lovingly created by the Creator. It is so beneficial for you to look at your body every day in amazement, and see what it does for you. Just look at your fingers and how they move to pick things up for you. Look through your eyes, and realize they are seeing the beauty of everything around you, as well as guiding you to walk with confidence. Look at the way your legs and arms move. See the way all your organs, muscles and bones work, the way your blood flows and how it all moves together for the highest good of the body, unless you compromise it with choices that do not serve you well. You can help and love the body and yourself with your deeper realization of all that goes on behind the scenes, in your body, on this planet and in the Universe.

There is a whole plan of action that works together out there, and all around you. It would be so beneficial for you to really understand this so you can be more joyful, loving and grateful each day for the many gifts that are already yours.

Where is there room for concern in all of this? As you can see, it pushes concern right off the map. It takes your attention and fills it with what you already have, leaving no room for what you think you don't have. You are no longer thinking you need more money to get those things. You are busy enjoying what is already yours. The prosperity you long for is climbing in the windows to get to you because you are vibrating so high from realizing how rich you already are.

The rule of like attracts like is actively at

work all around you. Let it in now, and see how much more enjoyable your life is, and how it flows together with grace and ease, in a way that you may not even imagine right now.

These actions are Acts of True Love for everything, not the love that is only written about on greeting cards, but the love that is written in your heart when you look out through your eyes and see the beauty all around you with wonder, and appreciation and love.

You are loved with an everlasting love.

FOCUS ON THE DIVINE

I asked the Beloveds about our relationship with the Divine and this was their reply:

Let us speak of the Divine, which lives and breathes in each of you, as you. Your physical body is like an empty shell until it is animated with the breath of the Divine/ God/ Source/ Creator.

It is a fundamental Truth that your body cannot do anything without that Divine Light energy within it, filling it and giving it the energy, the inner guidance and wisdom to do all that it does. If you thought about all the little nuances of the body, and how much is required to take place in Divine Timing and Divine Order, it would absolutely be beyond the mind to comprehend.

It is an amazing feat of the Divine within you, because no human mind could conceive of what it takes to make your amazing body work the way it does. This energy is all around you, operating in everything, the same way the sap flows in trees, the photosynthesis process between the light and the leaves of the plants and trees, the birds and bees; we could go on and on. But that is not necessary because you get the drift of what we are saying.

There is a Divine Plan behind everything, so the realization of that can give you the faith to know there is, indeed, a Divine Presence or whatever you want to call it. You could call it just pure energy. It is all the same, the great hand of the Divine, working it all together into a beautiful symphony. Sometimes this symphony gets out of tune because of discordant notes that happen within the symphony of life. This does not interfere with the Divine conductor behind all of it. The Divine is still there, conducting it all behind the scenes.

The key is to focus on the conductor rather than the discordant notes. The more you focus on the discordant notes, the more of that you attract into your energy field. How could it be otherwise? By focusing on the discordant notes, you begin to vibrate on that frequency, depending on how long you choose to focus in that direction.

Then it becomes cumulative, and you think you have a terrible life. All you see are the discordant places in your consciousness, which are destroying your peace of mind. But the beautiful life, the symphony, is still going on at the same time. You can choose to stop focusing on the discordant notes, a moment at a time.

You are consciousness, and that consciousness is all-knowing, so be protective of it by being aware of what you allow into your consciousness. Pay attention to where you allow your thoughts to drift, and how long you allow them to stay there.

Your well-being depends on how much time you are dwelling on all that seems not to be working in your life. That is one of the major keys to pay attention to. Really be aware of how you are living your life, and decide to make a change, if necessary. It is not something you can readily do alone, so ask for help from the Divine Conductor.

Old thoughts and ways of being that no longer serve you have sneaked up on you, a little at a time, and become part of your mind structure. It infiltrates everything you do, and thus your life can show up in a less than wonderful way.

Whatever is showing up in your life is what you have allowed your mind to dwell on, whether it is positive or negative. It is your choice as to where you allow your mind to drift. The longer you allow it to dwell on something, it takes a firm hold of your consciousness, and that becomes your vibration. Make a conscious choice to focus on what you want to attract into your life because the Law of Attraction truly is at work.

You are loved with an everlasting love.

USE THE LAW OF ATTRACTION

When I asked the Beloveds to share more about The Law of Attraction, this was their reply:

The Law of Attraction is truly at work in your life. You attract what your vibration is. Like attracts like. There is much out there that is truly beautiful of a high frequency, of a vibration that will insure your well-being.

There is also the opposite, which will have the opposite influence in your life from the low vibration. Life will seem like you are slogging through mud, and things don't seem to be working, and you find difficulties all around you. To the degree that you have focused in that direction is the degree it is showing up in your life.

How do you fix this? Think of it this way: these things that seem negative are actually positive, because you are now awake to the fact that something has happened to attract all this. It is not good or bad; it is just what you are experiencing, due to where you let your attention drift.

Actually, it works out pretty well because things start showing up rapidly to show you that you don't want to continue in that way. Use the Law of Attraction to your benefit and stop drifting into things that cause difficulty. Be aware and choose more consciously.

You are loved with an everlasting love.

GRACE IS NOT EARNED;
GRACE IS A GIFT

Let us speak to you of Grace. Grace is not earned. Grace is a gift. It comes to you like your breath. It is always there. It is about receptivity. It is about allowing. It is about breathing into it and being full of grace as you move through your life each day. That wisdom came from the Beloved Guides.

Sometimes life feels so full of what seems to be the opposite of grace... obstacles that make us wonder where the grace is. I have been reminding myself that these obstacles, that I wish I could get rid of, are opportunities for me to lift my vibration, and stay open to grace flowing in. I know it's there; yet when I am focused and overwhelmed by the circumstances around me, I can't feel the grace, and the obstacles seem to grow in magnitude.

I remind myself that whatever is there now is there because I attracted it for a reason. The reason is usually because it is an opportunity for me to experience something in a new way from a higher perspective than I may have before. Obstacles have a way of redirecting us to see the grace we may not have seen before.

Usually, the way I raise my perspective is to find something to appreciate. Nature really does it for me. It may be family and friends for you or whatever. My African violets are perfect for that, as I breathe in their beauty and let it fill me. I may not have seen the beauty and the grace because I was focused on the obstacles. It's a perfect opportunity to shift my focus.

This is a constant practice, because it's very easy to slip into old ways of being. We can practice shifting our focus about everything by seeing what else is there beside the obstacle. If it seems overwhelming, we can just be with it. We can be where we are, and love ourselves just the way we are, right where we are, and we can choose to be with people whose vibration is high until we can do it for ourselves.

PERSPECTIVE FROM
YOUR HIGHER SELF

Recently something happened that triggered me, and I could feel myself being upset around it, so I asked for guidance from the Beloved Guides. This was the Writing I received from them:

It matters not the charge or upset or degree of it. The person or situation you are having the charge around is being used as one more messenger showing you to yourself. As you view all this from your Higher Self perspective, you see one more place within you that can get easily disturbed, easily thrown out of balance because you see it as something you disagree with.

All your old beliefs and patterns are

coming up for you to see how attached you are to your way of viewing the world the way you think it should be, your own personal perspective of yea, yea, nay, nay.

Each time this comes up for your review, no matter what it is, it is an opportunity for you to see another belief you have about something that does not serve you or the world. You can all do yourselves a great favor or disservice, depending on how you continue to view everything that shows up around you. These occurrences are opportunities.

Do not choose to get blown away by the energy to disagree or disapprove or to resist what is. It is a waste of your precious energy best used for keeping yourself Whole as the One, rather than fragmented into little areas of belief in this or disbelief in that. There is so much good you can be guided to do from a higher perspective. It will call for you to see with your spiritual eyes rather than your human eyes. With this frame of mind and heart, what you choose to do will have a lasting effect and really accomplish something worthwhile. Many of your beliefs are based on old ways of being, on what you have been taught, and no longer serve you and the planet.

You can see where it has gotten all of you. It is brand new now.

Hold on and wait. Do not jump into this or that cause. Wait! Keep your energy field intact, for you will need it for the upcoming work of healing the planet and bringing about peace. Many systems are in breakdown mode, so be at peace in the midst of it, rather than wasting time and energy on every passing thing that comes your way. You have a mission. You all do. Remain at peace through all of it, through all the disturbances. Do not add your energy to disturbances. Stay intact. Stay strong.

You will receive instruction as you move along. Have no fear. Fear fragments your energy. You cannot afford to do that at this time. Your energy field is needed to keep the field of the planet as high as possible at this critical time. Many changes are in the works, which will unfold and will be shared with you when it is time.

You need not try to change anything or make anything happen. Be with it as it is, watch it, and watch yourself. No matter which side of an issue you are on, it is still a side, not the whole thing, and will fragment your peace. Make the choice not to choose sides. Choose love. Choose to stay in your Wholeness, and watch it all without becoming embroiled. This will serve you and the planet because the peace on the planet starts with peace in your own heart, and change will happen. Remember the work that Gandhi accomplished. Be the peace and love you want to see in the world.

You are loved with an everlasting love.

KEEP YOUR HEART FREE
OF USELESS EMOTIONS

Beloveds, I feel guilty because I chose to answer an email rather than coming directly to write with you. You said meet us here at 6:00AM and I always find some excuse to delay, causing myself to feel guilty that I'm late. Their response was:

Child of God, guilt is such a wasted emotion. It holds you back from the inner joy that is bubbling to the surface from within you. You open the door to joy by keeping your heart free of guilt, blame, resentment and on and on. You have no need for any of those useless emotions.

You have a belief in physical time but in spirit there is no time. We give you the time

6:00AM so you have something to aim for, not something to be enslaved by. You were moved by your heart to write to your friend and that is fine. We hold no malice, and do not hold you responsible for being late and holding us up. What do you think we are doing here? Our energy is everywhere.

When and if you tune in, we are here. When you do not, we are here. We are always here, whether you are tuned in or not, so tune in whenever it suits you, and be free of guilt and blame and resentment against yourself for not doing what you think you "should," which then flows over into your world.

There is no need to feel guilt. Everything is an experience to learn from and move on. When you see the opportunity in the experience and absorb it, then you are ready for a new experience. Then you move on from there. Some experiences you revisit many times to be with them again and again before you stop. It is why it is such a waste of time to hold others in a space of resentment, blame and judgment. They will learn what is right for them to learn. They are going at their own pace.

Releasing yourself and others from

judgment clears your energy field so your life can flow freely, filled with the joy that is always bubbling to the surface when you allow it. You really can't feel peaceful when you are feeling judgmental; you can remind yourself that you could see peace instead. Ask for help because it is not easy to accomplish alone, so remember you are never alone. Guidance and help are always available when you stop and tune in to listen.

You are loved with an everlasting love.

THE HERE AND NOW

I woke up thinking about being more in the present moment. Then I read Denise DeSimone's *Daily Dose* and it said, *"Your true home is in the here and the now."* - Thich Nhat Hanh

What clearer message could I receive this morning? I can see that often my busy life covers up the here and the now, so I don't have to be aware of what's under all the busyness. I'm sure many people avoid the here and the now through a variety of addictions, whether it's busyness or whatever their drug of choice is, so the underlying pain of life which is hidden in the subconscious does not have to be faced. Awareness is the key to life, awareness in the present moment. If we are walking around not in the present moment and unaware, we miss out on the beauty, as well as whatever it is we are hiding from.

Beloveds, what would you share with us today about that?

Their reply:

Awareness is the only way to walk through life getting the most out of it. However, the Earth can be a difficult place to be, and you cannot live here without some degree of pain. Some have more pain than others, depending on their circumstances. However, the way to handle it no matter the amount of pain, small or a lot, is all the same when it comes to handling it. As you all know by now, it only makes things worse when you avoid handling it through an addiction, including being so busy you don't have time for anything but skimming the surface and not absorbing anything fully. The way to be aware and go deeply into life is to follow your own breath within.

The simplest way, the simplest tool, is your very own breath. You cannot stop it. It is the life force within you that breathes you; so, as you follow your breath, you are getting in touch with that life force.

During the day, take many moments to tune in and follow your breath. As you focus on your breath, if you would like to, you can say something *like "I AM harmony, I AM love, I AM the Light"* or you can simply be in the stillness following your breath peacefully in a balanced and harmonious way. It begins to slow down the rapid pace of your thoughts and of your racing heart, and gives you a sense of peace that has long evaded many who race from one thing to the next without absorbing the beauty at hand.

You have a beautiful planet made for your joy and love. Appreciate her. Breathe in her beauty, feel it, absorb it with your eyes, through your very skin, and add your breath to the breath of the Universe. The Universe breathes you, so tune into breathing with it consciously.

With love and appreciation to all of you on planet Earth, for taking the time and energy to read this writing we bring to you. Stay tuned for more.

You are loved with an everlasting love.

PEACE UNIVERSITY IS
A WONDERFUL PLACE

A message from the Beloved Guides:

Children of the Universe, the Universe and beyond are where you have come from, and you come to Earth at a time in your existence where you take what you have learned before, and bring it to this earth plane. You add to the learning already stored within you through the curriculum of your present lifetime.

Your life here is a learning ground, a time for you to see what is within you. What comes up for you as you experience your life? The reactive mind can cause you a world of challenges, or you can learn to respond from the heart of love and peace so you live in a world filled with solutions rather than challenges.

For example, when you face a particular challenge, your life provides the curriculum for you to go to Peace University. What in every situation will bring you more peace? Ask yourself that question. Will you react from the anger level that comes up in you because something is not going your way or does not look the way you think it should? Or will you take a breath and ask yourself what will bring me more peace in this situation?

You can learn from these interactions, and live with a more peaceful resolution to whatever it is that is coming up for you to experience. You have this opportunity, which doesn't always look like an opportunity.

This is an opportunity because of what it creates inside of you, and also for the world at large. You see how it makes you feel. How does it make you feel? You are the anchor for peace where you stand, and it goes out from you to those around you and the world. It all starts with you and your life. The way you choose to live peace is the Peace University's curriculum you choose to experience. Peace University is a wonderful place to hang out and get your degree on this realm. Peace is actually a choice to be kind to yourself and others. You will have a happier, more fulfilling life and it will improve the quality of your health; definitely a win/win.

You are loved with an everlasting love.

THE HUMMINGBIRD LESSON

The thought (actually guidance from within) came to me that the hummingbirds would be coming soon and it was time to put out the hummingbird feeder and prepare the hummingbird water. I forgot about it. The very next day a hummingbird appeared at our back window. I forgot about it again. A couple of days later the hummingbird returned, and there was nothing for her. So, I finally did it. I hope she comes back again and does not give up on me. I asked the Beloved Guides about what I was to learn from this.

This is the answer I received from them:

Have faith; the hummingbirds will return, and you will enjoy them for the rest of the season. There is a very good lesson here. You can call it "The Hummingbird Lesson" and let it serve you well. It is about receiving guidance and following it in a timely manner. In this case, it would be acting on your guidance about the hummingbirds. When you have a thought to do something, do it as soon as it needs to be done. We have shared this with you many times.

The opportunity is there for you to hear guidance all the time. When you listen the very first time, it doesn't have to come back again. When you don't listen, it can have difficult ramifications. It comes back as an opportunity for you to become a stronger and clearer channel for Spirit to come through as you listen to and follow the guidance quicker. Doing it clears your energy field so you don't have this hanging around in your mind thinking that you have to do it. It wastes so much energy. When your mind is clear, you are more aware. You become a better listener and follower of your guidance.

The external is giving you the opportunity to actually see the guidance show up in your life. As you tune in quicker, your life is easier. At that point, you will be shown how to live your life with even more grace and ease in

Divine Timing and Divine Order.

There really is a Divine timing and order. Life does not have to be difficult. It can be easier when you tune in sooner and see the results in your life. Guidance is happening all around you all the time. There are Hummingbird Lessons everywhere. They just look different. They are people, places, books and so many other things that are constant reminders of what to do or not do. Listen sooner, so the guidance doesn't have to keep repeating itself, or keep getting more difficult until you listen. Life could be a lot easier this way.

Try it for the next 24 hours, and see what happens when you get a thought (guidance from within) about doing something, and you actually do it, even the tiniest thing. It will be a delightful surprise and make you smile.

You are loved with an everlasting love.

RESOURCES

Abraham-Hicks – Abraham's wisdom comes through Esther Hicks. Abraham is a group consciousness from the non-physical dimension, the energy of Source. www.Abraham-Hicks.com

Alison David Bird, C.Ht. & Lisa Wilson, L.M.T., *Marconics – The Human Upgrade* – evolution of energy healing; a wave of higher dimensional healing frequencies. www.Marconics.com

All Faiths Seminary International – offers professional training and support to spiritual interfaith leaders; trains and awards Ministers, Master's and Doctorate degrees. Rev. Patricia Conte-Nelson is ordained as an Interfaith Minister. www.AllFaithsSeminary.org

Barbara Marx Hubbard, *The Revelation – Our Crisis is a Birth* – inspiration to anyone who believes that human transformation is possible. www.BarbaraMarxHubbard.com

Denise DeSimone, *Daily Dose* – inspirational message delivered via email each morning. www.DeniseDeSimone.com

Dr. Norma Milanovich and Dr. Shirley McCune, *The Light Shall Set You Free* – armistice for healing humanity's heart. www.RadiantEnergy.ca

Ernest Holmes, *The Science of Mind* – key to power and personal peace; change your thinking, change your life. www.ScienceOfMind.com

Ho'oponopono (Ho-o-pono-pono) – ancient Hawaiian practice of reconciliation and forgiveness. www.Hooponopono.org

Jackie Woodside, CPC, LICSW, *Calming The Chaos, A Soulful Guide to Managing Your Energy Rather Than Your Time* and *What If... It's Time for a Change* – breakthrough methods that lead to becoming the least stressed, most productive person you know. www.JackieWoodside.com

John-Roger, DSS, *The Way Out Book* – practical guide to becoming more aware of your spirituality. www.MSIA.org

Myrtle Fillmore, *Healing Letters* – extracts from her letters to people throughout the world requesting prayer. www.UnityOnLine.org

Oneness Blessing, Oneness University – sacred school for spiritual awakening located in Chittoor District, Andhra Pradesh, India. www.OnenessUniversity.org

Rev. Patricia Conte-Nelson – officiates all celebrations of life on Cape Cod, Massachusetts, including weddings, memorial services, baby blessings and christenings. www.WeddingsInCapeCod.com

Sri Aurobindo Ashram – spiritual community practicing meditation and spirituality located in

Pondicherry, India.
www.SriAurobindoAshram.org

Thich Nhat Hanh – Vietnamese Buddhist monk
and peace activist living in Plum Village in the
Dordogne region in the south of France.
www.ThichNhatHanhFoundation.org

Uell S. Anderson, *Three Magic Words* – series of
essays aimed at revealing your power over all
things; learn that your thoughts are key.
www.Amazon.Com/Three-Magic-Words-Uell-
Andersen

Unity Worldwide Spiritual Institute – positive path
for spiritual living institute to license and ordain
Unity ministers and Unity teachers. Patricia Conte-
Nelson is licensed as a Unity teacher.
www.UnityWorldwideMinistries.org

Note: All the organizations mentioned above offer
many resources. For more information, go to their
web address.